A
Summer in Ireland

A
Summer in Ireland

by
Michael H. Pathe, C. Ss. R.

The CANTWELL Press
Madison, Wisconsin
1931

Michael H. Pathe, C. Ss. R.

PART I
A Summer in Ireland

The memory of my visit to Ireland is still very fresh in my mind, and I shall endeavor to live over again, for your benefit, those three gloriously happy months. But in order that you may the better understand what this vacation meant to me, let me take you back through the hopes and the dreams of the years that are gone by.

It was in the year 1910 that I completed my classical studies in the great Jesuit College of Mungret, Limerick, and went to join the Redemptorist Order in America. My home, at this time, was located in a little village called Carrigahorig, in North Tipperary. On the morning of August 27th, I said good-bye to all that was dear to me, walked up the hill on which the village grew, looked back at the scenes of a happy boyhood, received my father's blessing, and went away. I passed through a country whose every home I knew, on to Nenagh, the town where I was born. Here I took train for Limerick. At Mungret I said farewell to my dear professors. From Queenstown I left on the ill-fated Lusitania for New York. When a boy of eighteen leaves his native land he is old enough to understand what he is doing. Love for home and country has grown strong enough to make him feel the strange emotions that are tearing at his heart. If he is going to meet a relative or friend on the distant shore there must be some small relief to the pain of parting.

From my earliest years there was always a passionate love for Ireland in my heart, and when I stood on the deck of the Lusitania and saw the form I loved fading, ever fading back into the hazy distance, I tasted, for the first time, a sorrow as bitter as it was real. Nor was there any comfort at the end of the voyage. I was going to America a total stranger to a strange land.

But there was one thought that buoyed me up, one balm that soothed my troubled spirit, one chorus that sang through all my tears. It was the hope, then born, that I would some day return. Some day to see old Ireland once again! Some day to meet old friends! Some day to visit home and clasp in my arms those who made home so happy! Some day to roam back over old familiar scenes! Ah, some day! It was this hope that brightened my way to the West. It followed me for the twenty years of my exile. It came with me through my novitiate in the Order. It stayed beside me through my seminary years. It was born anew on the day of my ordination. It was laughed at as the dream of a visionary. It was crushed and often called futile—but it never died in my heart.

My first appointment, as a young priest, was in St.

Louis, Missouri. The World War had already broken out like a disease on the face of the earth. The story of Ireland's fateful Easter-week was on every tongue, and her fight for freedom found an echo in every heart. What glorious memories the lovers of Ireland in America must ever cherish of the noble efforts with which they seconded the cause of the old land! Who that lived then in St. Louis can ever forget the cheering crowds that gathered around platforms, in parks and public halls—the prayerful thousands that knelt before the Celtic Cross that marks the Fenians' graves—the multitudes who gathered in the Coliseum to welcome the representatives of the New Ireland? Who is there that does not remember the matchless eloquence of a Robert Emmet Kane—that American of Americans whose belief in the freedom of small nations was not a mere shibboleth—the golden-tongued Judge O'Neill Ryan—and that noble Priest whose love for Ireland was ever a shining example to us all—the Reverend Peter O'Rourke? To be associated with such men in such a cause, was an enviable privilege indeed.

Nor were our efforts confined to oratory. We gave generously of our wealth that the rebellion might continue, and the last vestige of tyranny might be wiped out from the land we loved. Then alas, came dissension and civil strife, and the hearts of Irishmen the world over were filled with sorrow. The strife ended. The cloud of sorrow lifted. The sun of peace shone out again, and in its rays were warmed the hopes and dreams of an exile.

My Missionary career had already begun. It was carrying me from state to state—from one end of the country to the other. The Missions brought me into close contact with hundreds and thousands of Ireland's children in America. I listened, again and again, to their expressions of longing, to their dreams of returning home —and it all seemed but an echo of the desire in my own heart—a desire that would not be overcome.

At last there came a day when a loving God saw fit to answer an exile's prayer. Ever enshrined in my memory shall be the morning when I received word from one of my Superiors that I was to be allowed to return to Ireland for a vacation. For twelve years I had been on the Missions. I had been trying to write a record for God and Souls, for my beloved Order, and for the land of my birth. It was out of the generosity of my Superiors that this great privilege was offered me. And side by side in my heart with the joyful memories that are mine of my trip to Ireland—there will always be a feeling of deepest gratitude towards those who made it possible.

PART II

"And I'll bless the ship that takes me To my dear old Erin's shore"

So it came about that on June 1st I boarded the White Star Liner—Baltic. As the graceful ship slipped out of the harbor, steered its way down the Hudson, passed the Statue of Liberty and went out into the wide open spaces that belong alone to God, a dream had at last come true, and the hoping and longing of twenty years were being fulfilled. There are feelings too delicate for expression. There are thoughts too sacred for words. The heart of man is sometimes so overcome by the power of surging emotions that it can only express itself in tears. And of what strange contradictions we are made! For months I had thought only of this day and the joy it would bring, and never imagined how, as I looked back at the shores of my beloved United States, the joy should be so strangely mixed with sadness. For the U. S. A. is my home forever—the field of my labors—the adopted Mother who took me so kindly to her heart. My life is hers, and every drop of blood in me would gladly flow to save her honor, and to keep her flag unsoiled.

That voyage on the Baltic was a glorious prelude to the story of happiness that was before me. It was the conviction of all on board that a more interesting or more enjoyable trip could not be imagined. From the very beginning until our last hour on that vessel every moment throbbed with happiness. Nothing that I could here say in the way of praise for the White Star officials of the Baltic would be adequate to their deserts. From the Captain down to the most commonplace worker on the boat there was nothing but courtesy and refined good will. One can very readily understand why the White Star Line is so popular on the ocean when he sees how it fosters such a delightful camaraderie. Not once did we hear any complaint on any score whatsoever.

I remarked particularly the generous attention given to Catholics in the way of facilitating the offering of daily Mass. Splendidly serviceable altars were erected in Cabin, Tourist and Steerage Quarters every morning. Two young Catholic stewards were detailed to serve the priests. I will say they were not only efficient altar boys but their very manner was a source of great edification to all. Officers were frequently present to see that every-thing was conducted smoothly and without embarrass-ment. And on Sundays, when other denominations held their religious services, the same courteous attention was shown to them.

We had four or five Masses every day, and so many

people received Holy Communion each morning that toward the end of the voyage we ran short of hosts. This, when announced, was a cause of great disappointment to the good people. But a way was found out of the difficulty. Three holy Nuns were in the habit of coming each morning from the Cabin because our time for Mass in Tourist quarters suited them better. They were very practical-minded ladies, for when I told them of our plight concerning the hosts, they went immediately to their stewardess and procured two flat-irons. They heated these irons, prepared the flour and water, and so proceeded to bake the hosts. Then, with real Irish ingenuity, they cut the hosts with their rings and supplied us with hundreds of particles. Now—lest pride should take possession of their good hearts, for they were praised very highly for their work—a severe humiliation was in store for them. They went to the upper deck that day, and sat down on a bench, no doubt to recite their rosary. The wind had torn away the sign which said "Fresh Paint," and the habits of the holy Nuns were very badly daubed.

Well, every day of that trip was filled with splendid memories. If only my voice could reach the ears of all our fellow passengers. I'm sure such names as Jones, the gentlemanly Welsh Purser, as Delaney—the ever-smiling

Chief-Steward, as "Scotty"—the rival of Harry Lauder, as Stoking—the entertaining Holland musician, as Jack —the master of the cups, as Father Grogan—the Prince of Priests, will bring back memories of the happiest voyage that could ever be made on the ocean. As for the ladies, I can only say that if a popularity contest had been introduced, all of them would have won first prize. Without distinction of creed or nationality we mingled together on terms of staunchest friendship. There is something about the ocean that breeds true democracy. Here was no offensive aristocracy of wealth, but the appealing aristocracy of true Christian charity. Here was no snobbishness, but real refinement. Here was healthy, sound, old-fashioned human nature. And I know that every one of those passengers, like myself, will often turn back to those days, and will send from a heart of gratitude, best wishes to the good old Baltic for her continued and ever-increasing prosperity. I may here add that I shall never forget the kindly interest shown to all Irish-American passengers not only by the English officers of the ship, but also later on by every official of the White Star Company with whom we had to transact any business.

When we started from New York we looked forward rather gloomily to eight days of voyage. Before we were half way over we were regretting that the days were passing all too fast. And when at last the Baltic sighted land, a feeling of lonesomeness came over us and we were sad.

N. B.: Since these lines were written God has called Father Grogan to his eternal reward. May he rest in peace.

PART III
Dawn on the Hills of Ireland

The last night on that ocean voyage was a rather hectic one. Word had been passed around that we were due to see the shores of Ireland about four o'clock the following morning. Have you ever stood amidst the crowds that line a city street to watch some great personage pass by? And have you felt the strange thrill that sweeps over the heart when along the line the word is passed—"he's coming now?" Then you have a faint picture of the sensation created in Irish hearts on the Baltic when official announcement sealed the good report. The Irish did not want to sleep, and I'm afraid very many of the rest could not sleep. Hundreds of us remained up all through the night. There were many of those hundreds who, like myself, had watched and waited through all the days and nights of many long years for the blessed sight that was coming with the dawn.

At first we were a gay crowd, full of song and laughter. But as the night wore on a strange solemnity possessed us. Someone recited a verse that touchingly described our feelings:

> "*Tis many long years since I saw the green island*
> *And bade her farewell with a heart full of care,*

And far have I roamed since in valley and highland
Where nature had lavished her favors most rare.
But gay as the bowers and fair as the flowers,
That bloom in strange lands where, an exile, I rove—
Still dearest and rarest and nearest and fairest,
Shall be the dear scenes of the land of my love."

The hours dragged on, as we watched through the darkness for the morning. There was a streak of light far over the ocean. We spoke in whispers now—the welcome dawn was coming. Slowly, as a curtain rises on a drama, the dawn rose over the hills. Majestically, as a conquering hero, the sun walked into the heavens. Stealthily, as one who senses defeat, the mist began to vanish. A dim form was appearing on the distant waters. Not even a whisper now, save the sobs of joy that broke over waiting hearts.

Another and another step—the sun had claimed the day! And there in her green and golden loveliness lay the Emerald Gem of the Western World, the queen of the waters, the Ireland of all our dreams.

> *"Blessed be God! but there it is—*
> *The dawn on the hills of Ireland!*
> *God's angels lifting the night's dark cloud*
> *From the hearths and homes of our Sireland!*
> *Oh, Ireland! isn't it grand you look,*

Like a bride in her rich adornin'
And with all the pent-up love of our hearts
We bid you the Top o' the mornin'."

The men amongst us stood bare-headed in the ocean-morning's cold, bare-headed, as men would stand in the presence of something sacred. Oh, Ireland! Did you see, that blessed morn, the love that lives for you in your exile-children's hearts? Did you read in our tears the story of our longing for you? Did you understand our happiness as we reached out our arms to embrace you? And I had last seen you twenty years ago—through tears. Through tears I again behold you; but now they are tears of joy. When I raised the consecrated Host that morning in my last Mass on the Baltic, 'twas over Ireland's green hills I raised it. And mine was but one of nearly a thousand voices that cried, "Thank God for this blessed day!"

After breakfast we secured our baggage, hurried and worried a whole lot more than was necessary, got in everybody's way, said good-bye over and over to friends we may never meet again, and lo! the tender was beside us to bring us home.

I have not told you that during the entire voyage I did everything in my power to bring happiness to every heart. The ship had honored me with the title of "Chairman of Entertainments." I only tried to be worthy of the honor. But through all my life I shall never forget the moment when I walked out on the gangway, leaving the ship. From the decks above, and from the tender below there went up a mighty shout that must have been heard far over the waters. It was hearty, and it thrilled me. For it told eloquently the gratitude of a thousand hearts for what little I had done to make their voyage pleasant. It was more than I deserved, but it cheered me, and I shall hear it, down through my years, when other memories shall have faded away.

And now we must leave the Baltic. She had carried us in safety and in comfort across the world of waters. Though some of us may never see her again, be assured our eight days with her shall be enshrined in our heart's fondest recollections. How graceful she looks! How faithful she was! Old warrior of the ocean—we love you—Good-bye!

PART IV
First Impressions

We landed in Cobh on the morning of June 8th.
Landing facilities in Ireland are anything but comfortable. The crowd—I think there were seven or eight hundred of us—was packed into a building like sardines in a
tin. For hours the work of unloading dragged on, and
when all the trunks and bags and suit cases were
piled up for customs inspection, the sardines had the
better of us for comfort. You wait inside the door until a
man carrying your baggage shouts out your name. Then
you take after him in a game of hide and seek. You trip
over bags. You run into people. You stop to apologize.
And, like a will-o'-the-wisp, your man disappears. All the
time you are inhaling clouds of good, healthy Irish dust.
If you preserve your patience you are a fit subject for
canonization.

However, there is one thing that helps you to be pa-
tient—that is the gentlemanliness of every Irish official
in the port. You never know how "a kind word turns
away wrath" until a pair of smiling blue eyes are turned
on you, and a soft Irish brogue answers your questions.

Here, within an hour after landing, we began to realize
that we were in a different world. From the busy, whirl-

ing, maddening streets of New York to the quiet, easy-going, restful life of Cobh is a whole book of revelations.

In America everything is rushed. We not only talk fast, we eat fast, walk fast, live fast, drive fast, die fast. Outside of the fact that our criminals are neither caught fast nor sent to jail fast, everything else is on the run. Speed is a religion with us; efficiency a by-word; system a hobby. In Ireland they live differently and better—I think.

We want to crowd all the living we can into a day. They seem to take all the living they can out of a day. The motto on our desk is "Do it now." In their philosophy of life, without any damaging procrastination, "Now" and "an hour from now" make very little difference. I noticed that some American travelers, at first, were wrought up over this, but they soon fell willing victims to that spirit which alone could give them a peaceful and a profitable vacation.

When all is said and done, however, the Irish American still clings to the belief that it would be to Ireland's greater interests if landing accommodations in dear old Cobh were a little more up-to-date.

Cleared at last, we went to the States Hotel for dinner. As we walked thither, filling our lungs with air that seemed perfumed by heaven, a company of Free State

Soldiers marched past us. If 'twere done for effect, 'twere well done. If the soldiers were only on a regular routine—part of their daily program—the effect on all of us was the same. They were Irish Soldiers. Red-coats paraded when we were here before. Now—we are in the Irish Free State. And the thought tempted us to shout aloud for joy.

At the hotel there was another gathering of Baltic friends. We were loathe to part with one another. There was plenty of bantering, nothing but smiles, a good meal, plans to meet here, there and everywhere—and then a farewell that sent us scattering all over the Emerald Isle.

It was June.

> "Dreamer, say, will you dream for me
>   A wild sweet dream of a foreign land,
> Whose border sips of a foaming sea,
>   With lips of coral and silver sand;
> Where warm winds loll on the shady deeps,
>   Or lave themselves in the tearful mist
> The great wild wave of the breaker weeps,
>   O'er crags of opal and amethyst?"

No! you have not pictured Ireland in that month of June. You have not told of the hills all aglow with bloom and blossom, nor of the cloudless glory of that summer's sky. I know that poets have sung of Summer in Erin. I know that artists have translated to canvass the matchless beauties that enraptured them. I could only stand speech-less and feel something of the awe of a soul suddenly transported into the garden of Paradise. The rivers that sang their way to the sea through the verdant valleys of Erin were but echoing the joy that rippled o'er my heart that first day in Ireland.

Home! That blessed word that had often set an exile dreaming! Home! That magic word that mingled in strange enchantment the sorrow of longing and the joy of hope! Home! That word so like to Heaven! Home! Home again in Ireland!

PART V
Alma Mater

My first stop was to be in the County Galway, at the little town of Portumna. I drove through Cork, Limerick and Tipperary. I passed by towns and villages, sleeping, it seemed, in a summer Sunday's rest. I looked upon mountains and hills clothed in emerald green, and dipped into valleys of shining gold. I learned why McCarthy wrote: "Ah, sweet is Tipperary in the springtime of the year." I felt that inspiration that moved a pen to write: "A little bit of Heaven fell from out the skies one day." As I passed into the Golden Vale, I understood, what books could never tell—why Irishmen smiled when they died for their native land.

Outside the City of Limerick a strange coincidence occurred. There on my left was dear old Mungret College. I would return to it later to visit the scenes of a thrice happy boyhood. Ah, surely, I thought, there will be no one there who would remember the handball champion of 1908. Along the road a priest was cycling toward Mungret. I stared at him, and imagined I knew him. We passed. Yes, it must be he. I turned the car and followed him. It was my old friend, Father Cahill, S. J. Was it not strange that he was the last one to whom

I said good-bye in 1910 and the first I greeted in 1929? Father Cahill was Moderator of the Mungret Apostolic School in those days gone by. From him the future Missionaries learned the true meaning of their vocation. From his zealous heart we drew our love for Christ and souls. His name is forever bound up with our golden memories of our Alma Mater. To me the noble Society of Jesus is something sacred because I had spent the happiest years of my life with Father Cahill. And in spite of the fact that I am its unworthy product, I am yet proud to assert that I have never since known a Missionary College that could compare with Mungret. Its sons are carrying the standard of Christ today in every land. Its record is a worthy page in the annals of Ireland's Propagation of the Faith.

I journeyed on to Nenagh. Although there were but few people here who knew me, the dear old town held sweet memories for me. Its every street was as familiar as if I had left home only yesterday. At the old Christian Brothers School I thought of all the playmates of years gone by. In my travels through New York, Detroit, Chicago and San Francisco I had met many of them. What a pity there is no record of the wanderings and deeds of the children of that great school!

I remembered Nenagh as a thriving prosperous place.

I remembered the Missions in the beautiful church, St. Mary of the Rosary. I remembered, too, the curse of the Red-Coats, and was very glad that chapter of Nenagh's history was over. I remembered the Poor House, and smiled to see it now in ruins. There beside the ruins of one of the marks of English injustice a splendid hospital is now erected. It is in care of the Sisters.

And if I have not written a long chapter on the Nuns of Ireland it is because I feel entirely unable to express my appreciation of their truly remarkable character. Whoever thinks that the service of God is gloomy and sad should visit a Community of Sisters in Ireland. So if I sang many songs for all the patients in that hospital in Nenagh, and if my action is to be interpreted as frivo-lous, I must put all the blame on the good Sisters who, smilingly insisted that I could not leave the building until I sang.

Ah, dear old Nenagh, how I loved to be with you, how I hated to tear myself away from you! Your army of Priests the world over love you. May you prosper ever, and may your children always be blessed. "A Roarin' Tipp from Nenagh" is a sobriquet of which no one need be ashamed. And here is one who is very proud of it.

There is the little village with the big melodious name of Carrigahorig. I had spent much of my boyhood there.

To the casual visitor there is nothing very attractive about this village. But to me it was the "open sesame" to a thousand pleasant memories. Up that hill we trudged our daily way to the school in Terryglass, to meet the children from Kilbarron and Ballinderry, to see John Scales, the good old teacher, and "read the day's disaster in his morning face." Ah dear! Ah dear! The school-house is there—the same as ever. Some of the old school-mates of nearly thirty years ago were now the owners of property in and about the village. And their little children occupied the places where we drew our maps, or labored through fractions, or gnashed our teeth at the name of the man who invented the decimal system. I went into the school, just one large room, and watched the children at their work. I wondered, did these children relish the respite caused by the return of a past student as we used to do long ago. There by the old-fashioned fireplace John Scales was wont to stand and, in his balmy moments, reveal to our wondering souls the beauties of Shakespeare. One day he was acting Polonius' advice to the departing Laertes. The turf fire was blazing, and a flame caught the tail of the Master's coat, and we had free time for the rest of the day. Outside, across the road, the old monastic ruins of Terryglass still echo to the shouts of happy children. But John Scales is gone—

God rest his soul!—and nearly all the playmates of other days are scattered far and wide.

Back to Carrigahorig. In that river, at the foot of the hill we played. It was our barefoot trail. We caught the speckled trout, we trapped the wild ducks here. On the old bridge we were wont to gather when the day's work was done—to hear a song or whisper the dark plot for a raid on an orchard, or some prank to torment a neighbor. By Joyce's barn, on the road-side, we danced in the sweet evenings of summer. Against the side of the Bridge House we fought our handball tournaments. From Flynns to Houghs we showed our prowess in cycling. In Donoghue's Mill we tramped the drying corn. Under the bridge we "Probed" for eels, or hid from an angry parent. Another bridge, at the north end of the village recalled a fading incident to my mind. In the barracks at Carrigahorig there was stationed a young policeman. He was in love with a maiden who lived in Lorrha. In order the better to establish himself with her parents the lad promised to supply a goose for their Christmas table. The promise was a rash one. The luxury was beyond his means at that particular time. Now there lived in our village a charming soul named Mrs. Salmon. She kept a great flock of geese, and was rightly proud of them. One day the young policeman, seeing the Salmon geese in the river, and recalling the promise and the prospects arising out of its fulfillment, decided somehow that necessity knows no law. The result of his decision was a report to the Sergeant of the barracks that a fine fat goose had been stolen. The young policeman was detailed to investigate the case. Of course the robber was never discovered. I wonder was restitution ever made. But I'm sure Mrs. Salmon, in her characteristic good nature, would gladly forgive the despairing lover. And here above, near Cleary's, is the waterfall that once in boyhood's fancy I had thought was one of the seven wonders of the world.

But the river is now smothering in grass—no children's busy feet are there to keep it down. The bridge is deserted, and the waterfall sings a lonely song. Old friends were there to greet me, and bid me welcome home. I fear they sometimes thought that America had changed me. Ah, they never knew how much I loved that village and its people, or how I always pray that its hearts may be ever united, as once they were, in the friendship of real charity. Through many lands its army of children is scattered today. I wonder, do they look back betimes to the poor old village that is fading, and recall the happy days that used to be?

Across the Shannon, on the Galway side, rests the

town of Portumna. Its clean streets and tidy homes, the well-kept stores and shops, the wide-awake and up-to-date methods of the people, the splendid academy, the public hall furnishing excellent amusement, and over all the beautiful church with its noble and civic-spirited Parish Priest and Curate—these are the signs of the time. These indicate what giant steps Ireland has taken toward that prosperity for which she has longed through the centuries, and which she so richly deserves.

Right here let me answer a question that must have arisen in many minds, to wit: "Are not the conditions under which the majority of the people in Ireland live rather pitiful?" For you must have read, in some of our American magazines, articles that labored to give you such an impression. You have pictured homes surrounded by filth and unsanitary within? The image thus presented is as false as the spirit which inspires it is base.

My journeyings from Portumna took me all over the Irish Free State. I have marked in red lines on a map the track of my wanderings. It has all the appearance of a Chinese puzzle. I visited homes everywhere, in cities, towns, villages and country places. And I assure you I never entered one home in Ireland of which the most meticulous taste could not approve. I visited the Clad-dagh in Galway, and homes through the distant West.

I smiled "God save all here" across the thresholds of houses that dot the coast line to the South. I rambled, a welcome stranger, into hundreds of homes in Tipperary. I stopped often for a cup of tea between Tralee and Waterford and up through Kilkenny and Kildare. I went from Dublin to Roscommon, and on to Westport in Mayo. And from the thousands of miles I covered in that never-to-be-forgotten vacation I came away with this conviction: There is more poverty and lack of cleanliness in one block of a tenement district in New York City than in the entire length and breadth of Ireland.

One of the first things to impress you in the old land is the neatness and tidiness of its cottages. The poorest thatched-roof home is enveloped in a riot of flowers. Many a white-walled cabin, in that month of June, was a veritable bower of roses. And within, all was "spick and span." Of course you will not always find those luxuries that adorn our American homes. But luxury is neither a necessary part of cleanliness, nor an asset in the making of a sturdy race.

I was standing one day in the lobby of the Gresham Hotel in Dublin. A gentleman, with a very decided English accent, said to me:

"You are an American?"

I answered politely that I was. It is rather disconcerting to meet people in Ireland who call us "Yankees" by way of a sneer, and as a reproach. But their number, thank Heaven, is very few.

"Have you been through the slums of this city?" he asked.

"No," I said, "but I should like to visit them."

We went together. He was a splendid character. He too had heard wierd stories of these sections of Ireland's Capitol. In our peregrinations we met up with a prominent Dubliner. We expressed surprise at not finding much similarity between the story and the reality.

"Ah," said our new companion, "there was a time when your stories had a foundation in fact. But the new government has changed all that." The New Government! There's a magic wand that has passed over Ireland, and has wrought many wonderful changes. But more of this anon.

PART VI
Poor Ireland

An Irishman said to me a short time ago:

"I would not care to go to Ireland and have to meet so many beggars."

Now, if there is anyone who should suffer from beggars in Ireland, it is the American priest. And mind you, they are quick to detect *him* over there. I had little trouble. In Dublin a few urchins followed me pleading for pennies, and because pennies are such large, clumsy things, I was glad to get rid of them. Two or three times in the land I was bothered by adult beggars. I was disposed to help them, but a sudden appearance of a member of the Guard caused my beggars to vanish like the witches in Macbeth. For begging is prohibited in Ireland, and the violators of the law are put in jail.

Let no malcontents persuade you that the Irish at home are destitute. I had a letter from an old friend shortly after my arrival in New York. This friend had labored with me in the campaigns of the A. A. R. I. R. He warned me not to tell the American people that the Irish are prospering. "For," he said, "everybody knows that prosperity is impossible under the Free State." Powerful logic!

But the question of emigration is still a vital one. For as long as thousands of young men and women are convinced that work in foreign lands is better than at home, Ireland will continue to feel their loss.

One of the greatest difficulties in this regard is the so-called "first letter" home from America. That letter paints in glowing colors the luxuries and comforts and, above all, the splendid salaries in the new land. And straightaway the youth who reads is filled with restlessness. He begins to dream of his fortune beyond the sea. Why cannot he too make a lot of money like the neighbor's boy who is sending home so much? Next thing you find his name on the quota—and he's "off to Philadelphia in the morning."

Aye, so it is. But the letter never tells of the sweat and the grime of the factories, of the hours of slavery under grinding task-masters, of Godless surroundings. No! They never tell of the profane and filthy language poured constantly into their ears, and of the temptations that stalk before them on the streets. And Oh—they never tell of the thousands of Ireland's sons and daughters who have found it necessary to pawn their Faith for the few paltry dollars they send home. How Ireland used to abhor the "Soupers" money! How much of it she is getting today!

I never went through Dublin City during my stay that I did not meet, somewhere or other, a parade of men carrying on their backs large posters bearing the sign "Out on Strike." It seemed that strikes were as fashionable as bicycles, as popular as ladies' cigarettes. Next to strikes came the ubiquitous half-holiday. I was in a very busy town one Saturday noon in Kerry. I dropped into a large, up-to-date grocery store. Sharp at noon the doors were closed, business ceased, everybody went out—it was the grocers' half holiday. That's all.

But the exodus from Ireland is felt chiefly in farming districts. And here perhaps the young people have reason to complain. The most unheard-of doctrine in Ireland is that a farmer father should pay a just wage to his grown-up sons and daughters for their work on his land. They plow and till and make hay and cut the corn and never receive a penny that they may call their own. The parents hoard the money. As long as this continues there will be an emigration problem. Even at that the number leaving yearly is growing smaller. May it go on decreasing until at last a hard-working nation of giants has brightened its lovely land into solid and lasting prosperity.

Stay home—Youth of Erin—stay home. No cruel government is robbing your land or crushing it today.

You weep over the blood poor Ireland shed in the years of her persecution. You are causing a sadder loss of her life's blood today when by thousands you leave her shores. Stay home and work. There's plenty of work in Ireland. Look for it—as the youth must look for it in America.

PART VII

"We'll sing of the sunny meadows,
And we'll sing of the flowing streams;
Of the glens that sleep in shadows,
That haunt us in our dreams;
Of the dancing rills, and the high green hills,
And the homes we ne'er may see.
Then here's to the homes of Ireland
With a hearty three times three!"

The Irish American poet will forgive me if I have changed his song. At a farewell party in Galway I sang it, and tried so to give expression to my unbounded love for the homes of old Ireland. Nothing in all my vacation fascinated me so much as the hospitality of the Gael. Any attempt at eloquence, when dealing with this subject must necessarily fall far short of justice. If you want to see any country at its best you must move amongst its common people. I am not making a distinction as between rich and poor. Many a wealthy home in Ireland was blessed by a spirit of hospitality as simple as it was real. The common people I refer to are those who live such natural, healthy lives that they are neither spoiled by wealth nor soiled by poverty. They are the princes and princesses of the land whether they be clothed in latest style from London, or in corduroys and calicos. Ireland is full of such people—and their homes are more attractive than the famed Lakes of Killarney. An Irish home is a world all apart from everything. You may have to bow your head to pass over its threshold. You may see it covered with a thick roof of straw called "thatch." It's only grand piano may be but an accordion. Over in an old-fashioned fireplace a little hill of blazing turf is throwing out its marvellous heat. Perhaps the luxury of electric light has not yet replaced the soft glow of the ancient parafin lamp. The kitchen is your hallway, reception-room, and dining-room all in one. The pictures that hang on the walls might not be called works of art, nor would they meet the approval of modern asthetic taste. They are old prints of Christ and His Blessed Mother—older by far than the oldest dweller there—fading souvenirs of the Faith that wrote a glorious history. The kitchen floor is made of concrete or "flags." The furniture is classic in its simplicity. That's a country home in Ireland.

But go you the whole world over—in the palaces of kings—in the gay halls of princes—in the massive dwellings of millionaires—and I defy you to discover there anything that can distantly compare with the warmth of love, the sincerity of good will, the whole-heartedness of welcome, the depth of generosity, the cheer of smiling

eyes, the attractiveness of unpainted beauty and the real-
ness of hospitality that beam from every corner of a little
Irish home. A hundred thousand welcomes to you—
every word of it is meant. The old turf fire is singing it.
Sit near the "hob" and listen to it. Even the dog puts his
head on your knee, and if he could speak, you just know
he'd say "I'm glad you came." The crickets start up their
tune of welcome. "You must have a cup of tea—'twill
refresh you." Don't refuse it, for a cup of Irish tea is the
Nectar o' the Gods. You do not know what tea is till an
Irish Mother makes it for you. Someone slips out of the
house and passes the word on to the neighbors. Soon the
crowds begin to gather. And when they give you their
hand they're giving you their heart as well. Come! Another
cup of tea. You may as well stay for the evening. James
has brought his "fiddle," and the O'Reilly girl has the new
concertina she brought down from Dublin. A song—
did you say? Sure, they're aching to sing for you. The
Irish heart has always told itself in song. Every noble
impulse, every sacred thought has music in Ireland. The
soul of the land is a delicate harp, and its strings vibrate
to every slightest touch. So, you go "Smiling along on the
jaunting-car." You travel the "Old Bog Road." You hear
the story of "Little Bridgie Flynn." You live back in the

days of "Old Phelim Brady." You wish you knew "Kelly, the boy from Killane."

Ah! Those songs of Ireland! Often now in lonely hours I think of them. How they rang through the country-side in dear old Tipperary! How they imaged the pure joy of the hearts of lovely Galway! How they told of an honest people's welcome in Kerry and Clare! How they shouted the old rebellion of Cork! How they throbbed with love in Dublin! How through distant Connemara they unfolded the pages of Ireland's ancient glories, or sang, in mournful strains, the story of her tears!

Oh—The homes of Ireland, how blessed and happy they are! No wonder God loves them. No wonder Mary has a special care of them. No wonder they have produced the world's bravest manhood and purest womanhood. Homes of Ireland—from my heart I bless you. Thatched-roofed homes of the country, I long to be back by your cheery fire-sides. Happy homes of the city I shall ever think of you. Hospitable homes of Ireland— Farewell!

PART VIII
Rambling through Paradise

For any traveler in Ireland to pick out one place as more beautiful than another is not an easy task. And to say that there are spots as entrancing as Killarney or even more so, is to go against sacred tradition itself. The world has been singing about Killarney's lakes and dells, and no one can go counter to the universal belief that Killarney is the loveliest spot in Ireland. Indeed, I, for one, would not attempt to steal one iota of praise from that garden of the gods. But I would have you understand that Killarney is only one of a thousand places in Ireland where angels entranced with natural beauty must "fold their wings and rest."

Quite naturally I think that a drive from Carrigahorig to Clonmel in Tipperary would furnish the world's greatest artist with themes worthy of his skill. Some poetess long ago wrote:

"Were you ever in sweet Tipperary
   Where the fields are so sunny and green
Where the heath-brown Slieve Bloom and the Galtees
   Look down with so proud a mien?
'Tis there you would find more beauty
   Than is on all Irish ground,

God bless you, sweet Tipperary!
For where can your match be found?

I think too that volumes could not contain an adequate description of the magnificence of scenery that presents itself to him who journeys along the West coast from Galway City to Belmullet in Mayo. Every turn of the road unfolds new wonders to the eye, and the soul is enraptured by the majesty of mountains, or filled with awe in the prayerful silence of the valleys.

But I would take you on another trip to show you a section of Ireland that needs no music to advertise its beauty, because it is a song of loveliness in itself. One golden summer day I left the city of Dublin, and followed the trail to Glendalough. The way lead out through Bray, the "gateway to the garden of Ireland," along the wide Stillorgan road. Here, as everywhere throughout the Emerald Isle, the American tourist is compelled to pay a fitting tribute to the new government for the ex-cellent roads it has built all over the land.

It was early morning, and as I turned out of Bray there before me rose the Wicklow Hills—peaks that melted off in the hazy distance. On now into the silence of an unspoiled and peaceful country where the bird and wildflower hold undisputed sway. To the left lies the great Sugarloaf Mountain—the sunlight dancing on its cone-shaped summit. A long stretch of hill leads past Roundwood and Dublin's reservoir. To the right Lugalla "the hollow of sweet sounds" and the sparkling Lake Dan are beckoning the visitor. But his objective is further on. Near the village of Laragh I was promptly jerked back from the dreams in which I thought I was living, from mysticism to materialism in one moment— by the crude reality of a flat tire. My saintly Irish Mother, two of my sisters, and TadgÓg, the brother, were with me. The best company in the world, but no help when a tire falls by the wayside.

All around us the rhododendrons were scattered in wild profusion, their vivid red contrasting strangely with the sombre colors of the pine clad slopes that looked over them. Away again—till we dipped into the valley of Glendalough. I confess I am utterly unable to describe that scene. I could feel the poetry of it, but I could not write it. Stand in contemplation near the upper lake— look over to the mountains that rise abruptly from the shore. Look down the valley dotted by the ruins of the Seven Churches. Conjure up in your mind the glories that once made Glendalough a household word all over Europe. And you will feel that words, mere words, would but mock your thoughts. Oh, Glendalough! treasure-chest of countless memories, with you is indissolubly linked the fame and sanctity of Ireland. Here the great St. Kevin spent a long life devoted to prayer and self-denial. Around him grew the Seven Churches whence the Holy Legion ministered to a saintly people thirteen hundred years ago. Around this sanctuary too, time has woven many legends. The boatsman who rows the tourists over to "St. Kevin's Bed" is well versed in these legends, and an hour with him is a veritable trip to fairy-land. His deep blue eyes—the bluest I have ever seen—had a roguish glint as he told his stories.

"Kevin was in love with a beautiful girl named Kathleen. But he decided to give himself to God, and spend his life in prayer. He was a wise young man, Sir, because there isn't much time for prayer when there's a woman 'round the house. So he came to this spot, and built himself a room in the rock over there. He thought Kathleen would never find him now. But he wasn't so wise after all, Sir, because no man can ever securely hide himself from the woman who loves him. So one mornin', when Kevin rose early to pray, lo and behold you! there was Kathleen in front of his hiding place. She was standing on the ledge of the rock. All of a sudden she heard a voice behind her sayin', 'What are you doin' here?' And the fright was so great she slipped from the rock, into the lake, and was drowned."

"Ah, poor Kathleen," I said.

"But she comes back, Sir. Oh yes. She comes back. Every night you can see her spirit over the waters."

We climbed the rock to Kevin's bed—thinking we might be following Kathleen at every step. Of course we "made a wish"—for legend says that every wish that's made in that rock-ribbed sanctuary must come true.

Rowing back over the lake the blue-eyed boatman told us that St. Kevin still cares for the people that live in Glendalough.

"Oh yes, indeed, for do you see those large white rocks up on the hill? Well, during the war the British refused to give us any sugar. And you know, Sir, a cup o' tea without sugar is no good at all. So the people prayed to St. Kevin, and all those white rocks were turned into big lumps of sugar."

When at last we had to leave I asked our entertaining guide how much I owed him for his kindness.

"Well now, Sir," he said, "you can give me anything you like. It was a pleasure to have such lovely people with me." He was clever, that boatman with the roguish blue eyes.

In fancy now I often return to Glendalough to dwell on its forlorn majesty, to see the sunlight on old Derrybawn, to hear the call of the wild birds, to feel the peace of soul that surpasses understanding.

The day is passing, but e'er it goes we must visit another spot. By the lovely vale of Clara to Rathdrum, our way leads down to the "Meeting of the Waters."

> *"There is not in this wide world a valley so sweet*
> *As this vale in whose bosom the bright waters meet.*
> *Oh the last ray of feeling and life must depart.*
> *E'er the bloom of that valley shall fade from my heart."*

Like a thousand voices blending in unison, the waters of two rivers unite in a valley of fantastic beauty. Castle Howard looks down from its sylvan eerie and is pleased. Near the river is a tree—a withered stump now—preserved to show the stranger where Moore wrote his:

> *"Sweet vale of Avoca, how calm could I rest*
> *In thy bosom of shade with the friends I love best."*

This tree was pointed out to us by an old man, and it seemed that no one had to point out to him the fact that we were strangers.

"Owen Kavanaugh is my name, Sir, and I've spent eighty summers and as many winters right here."

And Owen did not look to be a day beyond fifty. After entertaining us with a dissertation on Tom Moore he said: "But I never could understand why Moore spent so much of his time in England. Now the whiskey over there is not to be compared with the whiskey you can buy here."

"I like his poetry anyhow," I said, "no matter where he wrote it."

"Well," said Owen, "I think I could be a poet myself if I had a little drop. But these are hard times; and a poor man . . ."

If Owen isn't writing poems to-day it's not my fault. For he was in excellent spirits when we left him.

We went on to Woodenbridge—to see the second meeting of the waters. It was evening. Away in the West the sun was setting, its fiery orb tinting the land-scape with gold. It hung on the horizon as if loathe to leave such splendor. Wafted through the ghostly mist, on the soft, pine-scented breeze, came the hushed voices of birds—a kind of benediction from nature to the Master Hand that painted Ireland so.

And deep in my heart is a prayer of thanksgiving that I once more have seen you, Oh, Ireland! You have cheered my labors and lighted my way in a foreign land, and the new memory of you must ever spur me on to such tasks as will make me less unworthy of such a Motherland.

PART IX
Catholic Emancipation

One hundred years ago there was great sorrow in Ireland. Centuries of misrule, prior to this, had brought the Irish people to an abject condition of servitude. "The masses seemed to be rooted in helplessness," says a historian. To anyone who reads the story of the Penal Laws it must be a surprise that the Irish Nation continued to exist at all. Edmund Burke said that those Penal Laws, laid by England on the Irish people, were "as well fitted for the oppression, impoverishment and degradation of a people, and the debasement in them of human nature itself, as ever proceeded from the perverted ingenuity of man." All this because Ireland was Catholic and her people refused to exchange their Faith for the Established Church whose Pope was an English King.

But one hundred years ago Daniel O'Connell, with a united Ireland behind him, stood before his country's oppressor, and demanded Catholic Emancipation. Like Moses he led his people out of bondage. And so it was that on the Centenary of his great victory over injustice a grateful nation gathered to do honor to the "greatest Irishman that ever lived."

To spend a holiday in Ireland during the summer

months of any year is most enjoyable. But to be an eye-witness to the great events that transpired there in the summer of 1929, is I think, one of the greatest honors that ever thrilled an Irish heart.

For a long time Ireland was making ready for the anniversary. On June 22nd the key-note was struck, and the entire land burst forth in a song of gratitude and joy. Prayers were offered in every church that fine weather might grace the opening celebration. Every citizen of Dublin on that twenty-second of June will remember how, in the very early morning, the sky was dark and threatening, and how again, as the hours flew on, the clouds began to break, and hopes brightened with a brightening day. By noon the sun was in undisputed control.

From Ranelagh to Phoenix Park is not a short walk, but it gave me a better idea of Dublin in gala attire than I could get from either a street-car or a taxi. The streets were literally packed with people, not a riotous, disorderly crowd, but a solemn-visaged, serious, rather quiet mass of men and women. One could tell, as he moved along, that all the counties of Ireland were represented there, just as we could tell in America, nine times out of ten, by the accent peculiar to this place or that.

Down the main streets and along the side streets the

people moved. The Quay was our objective. And along the Quay we marched to Phoenix Park.

The City of Dublin was decorated that day like a wonderful shrine. From house to house, across the streets were banners bearing such inscriptions as "God bless our Pope", "Faith of our Fathers—we will be true till death", "Welcome Christ." Each home was festooned with garlands. The Papal colors floated everywhere, side by side with Ireland's beloved Tri-color. In the so-called slum district especially, neighbor vied with neighbor in the artful adornment of the homes. So attractively decorated was this particular portion of Dublin that an English Bishop said to me the following day: "'Tis in the hearts of the poor, no doubt, that Ireland's love of Christ is at its best." Yes, your Lordship, and the same can be said of the Irish the whole world over.

In Phoenix Park we quickened our steps till we came to what is called "the fifteen acres." At the far end of this green-carpeted space an altar was raised. It was a masterpiece of construction, and was plainly visible from all parts of the field. The crowd kept pouring in. It was nearing the time for Holy Mass. Over half a million people had already assembled. There was a special place allotted to each County, and here, for the first time, I marked the extraordinary efficiency of the Civic Guards, the new Police force of the Free State Government. They did giants' work in keeping perfect order in that vast area. I was to meet and mingle with and love them later on. I certainly admired their discipline that day. A special place around the golden altar was reserved for the clergy, but because I wanted to see what my eyes may never behold again, I preferred to move freely about the grounds.

I saw devotion such as I never witnessed before. I saw a million eyes lifted in Faith to one altar and one God. I saw the kneeling multitude that gripped my heart. I saw Ireland prostrate before the only King she ever acknowledged. I had seen the Mammoth Congress in Chicago, marvelled at the greater numbers, gasped at its golden magnificence, was carried away by its attractiveness and splendor, but—though comparisons are odious—I did not think, it could compare with the outpouring of Faith I witnessed that blessed day in Dublin.

Above was Ireland's bluest sky. Beneath was her brightest green. At one part of the Mass a flock of white doves hovered over the field, then passed out of sight. Instinctively you felt that Ireland's martyred heroes of the centuries were looking down upon that scene—that their spirits, like the doves, were hovering near. And when the bugles announced that Christ was present on the Altar, you knew that there in that glorious open-air cathedral the Irish saints of all Europe were looking down with pride upon the multitude bending in lowly adoration.

When Mass was over I left the park to search for a place where I could best view the procession. All through the day I was in the company of the great Father Grogan of New York, one of the noblest and most zealous Irish Priests in America. It is he who for twenty-five years has taken such interest in the Irish immigrant that his services have become indispensable to the steamship companies, and a Heaven-sent benediction to hundreds of thousands of Irish boys and girls. We stopped at King's Bridge, at the end of a long, straight stretch of road that leads down from the entrance of Phoenix Park. Here thanks to the inveigling ways of Father Grogan, we were privileged to stand between two soldiers and had an undisturbed view of all Park Gate Street.

Military bugles announced the coming of the procession. The military band lead the way. Then for three hours we watched the manhood of Ireland passing by. Oh, that I could rightly picture that thrilling sight, or translate into words the feelings that surged in my heart as I stood and watched.

Down the wide street came the men of Ireland, eight abreast, the finest body of stalwart men the world could ever behold. Down they came—marching for Christ. There were the giants of the South, the serious faced men of the North, the low-sized but hardy men of the East, and the gaunt, brawny natives of the West. Down they came, singing, praying, marching—for Christ. It was a victorious march. For centuries their priests were hunted, their Mass proscribed. For centuries their trust in God was a thing of scorn. Hewers of wood and drawers of water now no more, the men of Ireland marched that day in June and freedom rested on their brows. I saw old, grey-haired men in the ranks—keeping step with the youth of the land—marching, marching, marching,—for Christ and His Faith.

Near the end of the procession I turned aside and entered the Michael Collins Military Barracks from whose walls, overlooking the Quay, I could view the colorful march of the clergy. The members of secular clergy, the members of the religious orders in their distinctive garbs, the teaching Brothers, just a speck in that long, long procession of heroes who have passed through the most glorious pages of Ireland's history.

Now the Blessed Sacrament was approaching. The throngs of onlookers joined with the marchers as they filled the streets on both sides of the Liffey. On the Wattling Street bridge Benediction was given. In the center of the bridge an Altar was erected, and in such manner that all the people could see what was taking place.

The last hymn was sung, and the Blessed Sacrament was borne back to the chapel in the Barracks where I was then staying. The canopy over the Sacred Host was borne by government officials. President Cosgrave and Mr. De Valera—whatever in the past their political differences may have been—were now at least united in their devotion to Christ, their King.

As soon as the Sacramental Savior arrived at the outer gate of the Barracks, the body of soldiers in possession marched out by another gate. It was a very simple ceremony, and only a few of us witnessed it. And yet when the memory of all other events has faded in my mind, the impression made by this incident shall still be very fresh. The power of earth gave place to the Majesty of Heaven. The armies of men went out when the King of Kings came in. When later on I returned to America and called on Father Grogan in New York and talked over all our wonderful experiences in the old land, I was not surprised to hear him say:

"The most thrilling moment of all our vacation was when you and I knelt in the square of Michael Collins

Barracks and saw a Catholic nation standing aside for Christ."

So the greatest day in Ireland's modern history was over. A new chapter of her glories was written—and between the lines I thought I could read this message: "The past is dead. The bloodstains that defiled the fair face of Erin are blotted out. The sad dissensions of yester-years are ended. Our Faith has survived in the storm. And here around our only King we are united once more and forever."

It was a day never to be forgotten. It was Ireland's challenge to the world that she can never die.

The following Sunday I attended the celebration of Holy Mass in the ancient monastery on the Rock of Cashel. I stood in the sanctuary close to the Archbishop's throne. I saw the old walls alive with men. I saw the throngs that knelt on the Rock. I saw the upturned faces of the crowds on the plane below. I saw again the huge banners that floated in Gaelic "A hundred thousand wel-comes to Jesus and Mary!"

I heard the eloquence that poured out like gold. I stood close to Ireland's pride when he sang, with Ire-land's voice, "Sweet Sacrament, we Thee adore." How often through the cities of America John McCormack brought us back in fancy to the land across the sea! How often by the magic of his voice, he drew tears from our very hearts! But in "Cashel of the Kings" he was not just the singer of sweet songs, for with hands devoutly joined, and eyes closed in veneration, this noblest type of Catholic Irish gentleman was the very embodiment of Ireland's sweetest traditions.

So the Centenary of Catholic Emancipation was celebrated all over Ireland.

PART X
Ireland's Faith

Visitors will tell of the material progress of the new state—will describe the wonders of the new electric plant at Ardnacrusha—will recount the progress of a splendid government toward the reconstruction of a war torn land. But while I thank God for all these things I glory more in the knowledge that neither past irregularities nor modern progress have tampered with St. Patrick's sole and proudest heritage to his people—the Faith of Ireland.

This is the glory of Ireland—her Faith. This is the power of the Irish—their Faith. It is written that the ancient Irish, alone among the pagan nations, accepted the doctrines taught them by St. Patrick without the shedding of blood. That is true. Christ's coming to Ireland was another Bethlehem. The shepherds came down from the mountains to adore. The Kings gathered to lay their wealth at the feet of the Savior. And the hill-top fire of Tara was the star that guided them.

A few centuries more and Ireland became another Savior. Her children preached Christianity to the nations. There is hardly a country in Europe on whose altars the names of Irish Saints are not venerated. It could be said of Patrick's followers that they "went about doing good." But as with Christ so with those who love Him. Gethsemane and Calvary must follow Bethlehem. Then there came upon Ireland a fearful agony of seven hundred years. The world cried out against the cruelty of England, and said, "I see no harm in this just nation beside you." And England's answer was "Crucify Ireland." "Why, what harm has she done?" asked the world; and England shouted: "Away with her. Away with her Priests— away with her children—away to the gallows—away to slavery—Crucify her." And the true historian must relate that if Ireland had sold her birthright, had pawned her Faith for the inheritance of the Established Church, none of this persecution would have taken place. But even in the darkest hour of her Calvary, Ireland remained true to the Faith.

You who visit Ireland, whether you be Catholic or Protestant, must first understand their Faith before you can hope to understand the Irish people. Their Faith is their very life. They live with God in Ireland. They talk of God in every conversation. All things are referred to God. If the weather is bad or the crops a failure, they will say, as they tell you, "Praise be to God." Or if they rejoice over any success they never forget to add "thank God." They greet you with God's blessings. They part with you the same way. To the laborer in the field I shouted "God bless the work," and received again the answer I had often in childhood heard "God save you kindly."

To the old Mother in Lavally, in the County Galway, I was offering my sympathy in her sorrows. She merely pointed to a picture of Our Mother of Perpetual Help and said, "Sure, she suffered more than that, and why should I complain." It was no studied answer. It came from the fullness of Faith in her heart.

Every little home in Ireland is a shrine, where Christ and His Blessed Mother live. Every page of Irish history is colored by the nation's Faith. Every phase of Irish life is sweetened by that fidelity which has compelled the world's admiration and conquered all opposition. Oh, children of Ireland in America! You who have sold your birthright. You who have bartered the Faith for temporal gain—a mess of pottage! Could you but go back to the old land and see how you have proved traitorous to her centuries of blood, how costly your prosperity would appear! Could you but measure your loss by the content, ment of the Faith of your people you would surely sacri, fice all things to regain that same Faith from your God.

After the Mass on the Rock of Cashel, I went with friends to Thurles. Here the big-hearted owners of the

"Munster" gave us rest. Before sleep stole on our tired eyes do you wonder that we prayed: "God guard forever and keep unsullied the glorious Faith of Ireland."

> *"Lift up the drooping head,*
>   *Meehal Dhu Mac-Giolla-Kierin:*
> *Her blood yet boundeth red*
>   *Through the myriad veins of Erin;*
> *No! No! she is not dead—*
>   *Meehal Dhu Mac-Giolla-Kierin!*
> *Lo! she redeems*
> *The lost years of bygone ages—*
>   *New glory beams*
> *Henceforth on her history's pages!*
> *Her long penitential night of sorrow*
> *Yields at length before the reddening morrow!"*

PART XI

Shadows Departing

That Ireland is in a very healthy condition, spiritually and temporally, was the impression I carried back with me to the United States. Of the political situation I have not much to say. I followed the advice of my elders, and kept far away from all discussions on that matter. Furthermore, from what I did see and had to hear, I only became more established in my belief that a priest who puts his hands into politics draws out only badly burned fingers. The late political upheaval in Ireland belongs to history.

There were trying times in Erin. A nation rose up in arms against its ancient enemy. Feeling ran high. Bloodshed was the order of the day. Young men and women were carried away by the ideal of freeing their country. Patriotism burned in their hearts. The smoke of battle is cleared away now. Ireland has emerged a Free State, with her own government, her own army and her own police force. She is very happy and already the world has been astonished at her marvelous progress.

Although we ourselves participated in our own way in the struggle for the supremacy of the Tri-color, we can now calmly look back over the field and while we glory in the triumph of the cause, and wish that glory would ever increase, we must sadly regret the mistakes that were made in achieving that end. That blood was poured out—that tears were shed—that hearts were rent—sometimes without cause—cannot be denied. We regret it and grieve over it—even while we glory in the triumph Ireland at last has gained.

From all I could learn the people of Ireland have turned their backs to the past, are anxious to forget the orgy of blood, and have faced with bravery and confidence the development of their country.

The Free-State Government is now functioning with an efficiency that is truly exceptional. Youth and inexperience raise no obstacle whatsoever. We listened to Mr. Cosgrave during his visit to America, and he convinced us, beyond the shadow of a doubt, that as long as the cause of Ireland is in the hands and hearts of such men as he, its destiny amongst the nations of earth is very secure. We listened in Ireland to the praises of the people for the new government, and saw in that mutual confidence inevitable progress and assured prosperity.

The Free-State Government is of a very high order—its members are men of honor. It is very just in its dealings with the people. The Free State army is made up of a body of young men whose esprit-de-corps should be an outstanding example for the armies of the world. Splendid gentlemen all of them, clean-cut, upright, self-respecting men. The very neatness of their uniforms fills you with respect for the majesty of the Government they serve.

I must tell you a little incident that occurred during my vacation. On my way from Dublin to Galway in one of those comfortable busses that have now united all the towns and cities of Ireland, I met some of the soldiers. They were returning to the Barracks at the Curragh. One of them, although very sensible, was still suffering from the effects of some country wine. He acted very respectably toward me, and I might never have noticed any difference between him and his companions had he not felt it incumbent upon him to make some apology to me.

"You're all right my boy," I said, "Don't worry."

We reached the Curragh. The boys got out, and my young friend showed a slight stagger in his step. Standing close to the bus was a huge man with a red band around his military cap. An "M. P." sure enough. The young soldier saw a nasty situation, when he realized that a pair of questioning eyes were scrutinizing him from under the red band. His decision was instantaneous. He turned and hurried back to the bus—came to me—put his arm around my shoulder and told me something about a priest friend of his out in America. Then he shook hands with me as if I were his own brother. As soon as he stepped out, the bus pulled away. The "M. P." saluted me, and the last thing I saw was my soldier boy with a handkerchief to his eyes and evidently crying. For minutes I couldn't understand it all. Then it dawned on me. The only hope of clemency the boy had and his only chance of being passed up by the military policeman, was to convince this gentleman that he was saying a long farewell to his brother, or his cousin, or his something— the priest from America. It was a good ruse and I hope it worked.

While my associations with the soldiers were limited, though very pleasant, I met the members of the Guard frequently and those meetings all over Ireland form some of the finest memories I possess today. The Civic Guard is made up of the very truest and best men of Ireland. The successors of the Royal Irish Constabulary, they have fallen heir to the strict discipline and splendid spirit of what the British Consul in Detroit recently and rightly termed the "best organized body of policemen the world has ever seen." It was once written of the Irish Constabulary that ninety-nine per cent of the men were upright, godly men—the one per cent somewhat scoundrelly. For this one per cent hundreds had to pay the penalty of death, and hundreds more were forced to seek safety in exile. It was Ireland's loss.

It was most edifying to notice with what high respect the people treat the Guard, and how in turn the members of the Guard are kind and considerate toward the people. I was present in Dublin the day the Chief of Police of Paris reviewed the Civic Guard in the depot. And if you ever watched the policemen of New York marching down Fifth Avenue, and then saw that review in Dublin, you would not say that all the splendid men of Ireland had left the country. Of course it was not like the old parades in the Depot—it lacked the snap and precision and the formalities that grace the uniform. But never mind, for a new police force it was wonderful. I take off my hat to the Irish Guard. I'll always lovingly go back to the happy hours I spent with them. In old Kildare they treated me like a brother. In Dublin they were kindness itself. My last day in Dublin I violated some traffic law unwittingly. A great giant of a man put up his hand and stopped me.

"Now, Guard," said I, "Don't scold me, I'm leaving Ireland in a day or two and it's bad enough."

"All right, Father," was the quick answer, "Be on your way and may God bless you."

In Galway, amongst the Guard, I met some of the most

courteous and refined men who ever honored a uniform. In Thurles and through Tipperary, it was the same happy experience. All hail to you, Gardai Seacana!

PART XII
An Exile's Tears

My vacation was coming to a close—all too soon. Through the dreamland of Killarney again, through the mighty electric power plant at Ardnacrusha, once more through the verdant hills of Tipperary, and I was on my way to Dublin to say the good-bye that may be my very last in life. "Nothing begins and nothing ends that is not paid with moan." A great, true-hearted brother, and three adorable sisters and their splendid families—I can see them now as in those last moments smiling through their tears to make me brave. You did more than anyone else to make my vacation the blessed memory it is. Best brother on earth, and dearest sisters—Farewell!

My ship was to leave Galway on September 4th. Here is a harbor that in time will rival the very best. Its natural opportunities are immense. In a few years you will find that the popular place of landing and embarking will be dear old Galway Bay. You may have noticed, that I have a special place in my affections for Galway. Yes, I have, and I owe this to the exceptional generosity of its people, to my own dear relatives in Portumna and Galway City, to the people of Lavally, Fort Brown, and Mahanagh and the hundreds of real men and women whom I met. I think I shall never meet their like again.

Have you ever stood on an Irish dock and watched the scene of parting? Oh, it is heart-rending. A rather silent, tearful crowd assembled there. Soon little groups begin to form as each exile is surrounded by relatives or friends. A Mother is giving her last advice to her boy. A brother is crying the farewell to his lovely sister which she shall hear in her dreams for years. The exiles can only say "We'll come back soon to see you." And we know in our hearts that while some of us, please God, shall return, for others that "soon" means only when our hearts shall be united in eternity. Near us some one is playing a tune that tears our hearts: "Come back to Erin." Oh, were it not more merciful to leave without such a scene? The tender is waiting. The ship is out in the bay. The whistles blow, and the exiles go aboard. Slowly the boat passes out from the shore. Through tears we look back to the ever-receding vision. Oh, Ireland— our hearts are sore, our souls are filled with pain.

Two members of the Guard—faithful to the last— and some of my charming cousins came as far as the ship. Night and the darkness set in. Then the last adieu—and our faces were turned to the West.

Through a wall of darkness we see the fading lights of

the tender. Through a wall of darkness we send out our last, long farewell and our hearts best blessing to holy Ireland. Through a wall of darkness our tired eyes peer till the least flicker of a shore light is to be seen and the wall of darkness circles around our hearts.

It is good that the night is upon us; it is good that there are no more heartbreaks; it is good that there can be no more tears; it is good that we trust to the silence of the night the last song of a lonely heart—

> *While we gaze upon thy shore,*
> *That we never shall see more,*
> *And our blinding tears flow o'er*
> *We pray:*
> *Mavourneen be thou long,*
> *In peace the queen of song,*
> *In battle proud and strong,*
> *As the sea.*
> *Be Saints Thine offspring still,*
> *True heroes guard each hill*
> *And harps with every rill*
> *Sound free.*

MICHAEL H. PATHE, C. Ss. R.

If This Book should chance To Roam
And if perchance you find it.
Remember 'Marie is my name
And Murphy comes behind it